Surgery through time

Written by Anne Rooney

Contents

 Collins

Introduction

It's common now to have surgical operations to fix things that go wrong with our bodies. You probably know someone who's had an operation – you might even have had one yourself. If so, you've already come across modern surgery. Many operations are very simple and quick, and the patient recovers very quickly.

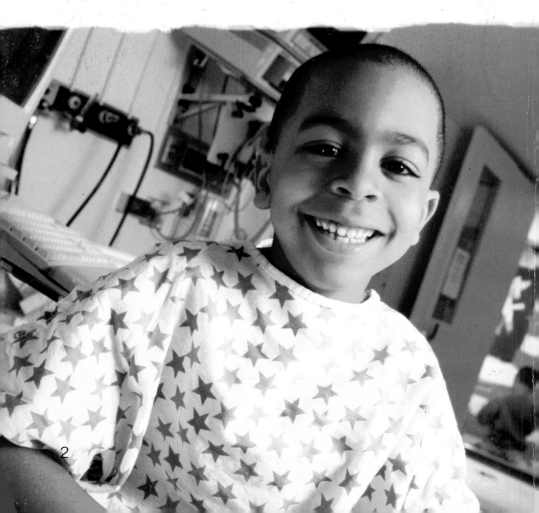

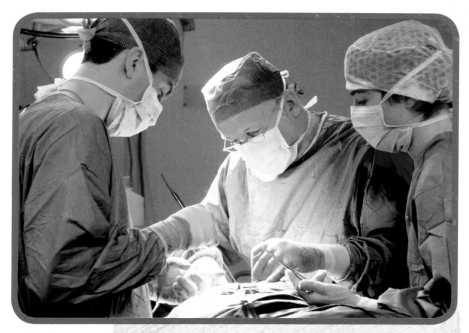

Anaesthetics and medicines make modern surgery painless and safe.

Now ...

Most surgery involves cutting the body to remove diseased parts, or to mend or replace damaged parts. You'll have an anaesthetic – an injection or gas that stops you feeling any pain. The hospital will keep everything clean and give you medicines to make sure you don't get an **infection**. A cut made for the operation will be stitched up so that it heals quickly and easily.

But it hasn't always been like this.

... and then

Just 150 years ago, illnesses and injuries were often deadly.
Even a broken arm or a nasty cut could kill you.

Long ago, operations could
be very painful.

People knew little about how the human body works, and nothing of the germs which cause infection. They had no anaesthetics or medicines to stop pain.

Old-style operations sound scary: digging out objects stuck in the body, cutting off damaged arms and legs, and even drilling holes in the skull – all without painkillers.

For thousands of years, there was only very basic surgery to help anyone injured in wars or accidents.

Tools for the job

Making a hole in someone's skull is called trephination. Thousands of years ago, trephination tools were stone knives and animal teeth attached to handles. Trephination might have been used to treat bad headaches. Now, a surgeon who needs to make a hole in the skull to operate on the brain uses a special metal drill.

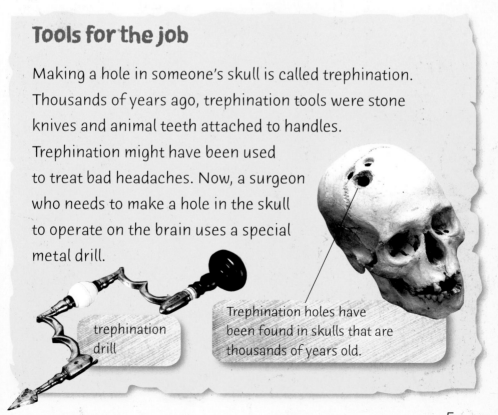

trephination drill

Trephination holes have been found in skulls that are thousands of years old.

Painless surgery

Early surgery was very painful. Surgeons worked quickly, with the struggling patient held or tied down. Sometimes patients died of shock. People would put up with a lot of misery rather than risk surgery – some even chose to die instead.

An anaesthetic is a chemical that stops a person feeling pain. Long ago, people used alcohol and drugs made from plants to try to numb pain, but these are not strong enough to deal with the agony of surgery.

Before anaesthetics were discovered, even having your teeth pulled out was agony.

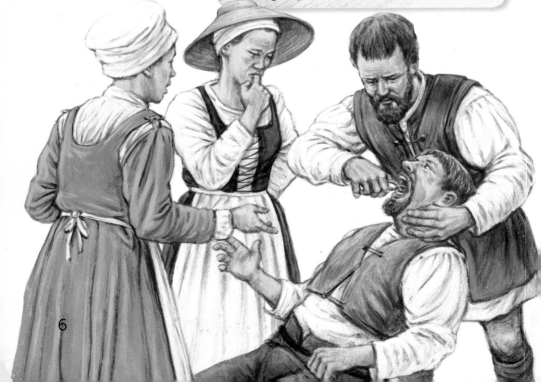

Without anaesthetics, surgery on the inside of the body was not possible – surgeons could only cut off limbs, remove objects such as bullets, or carry out simple tasks such as removing **tumours** or teeth.

Tools for the job

Early surgeons had large and small saws and knives for cutting through flesh and bones. They used pincers to pull out bullets and arrowheads, probes to search wounds and scissors to cut skin. Modern surgeons still use some similar tools, but they're better made – and cleaner!

Years ago, surgeons stored their tools in a wooden chest.

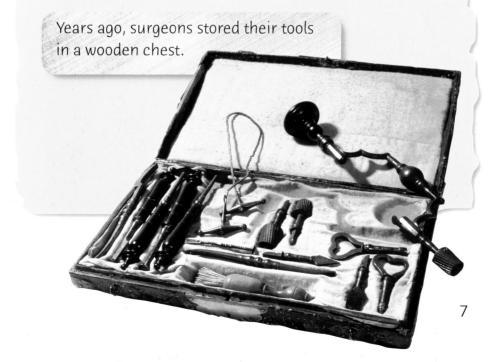

When doctors discovered anaesthetics in the 1800s, they could do longer, more complicated surgery. Under anaesthetic, the patient's muscles relax, making the surgeon's work easier. Many anaesthetics put the patient to sleep. These are called general anaesthetics.

The first modern anaesthetic was ether. It was used in 1846 by an American dentist called William Morton. Ether is a liquid which **evaporates** easily. Breathing in fumes from ether sends someone into a deep sleep.

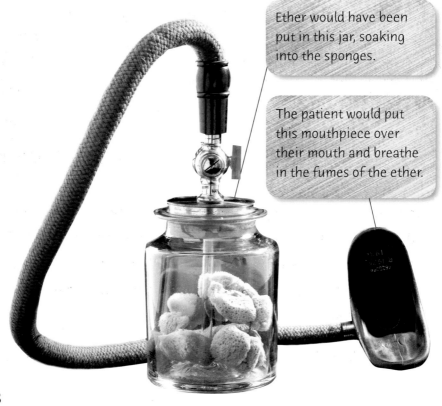

Ether would have been put in this jar, soaking into the sponges.

The patient would put this mouthpiece over their mouth and breathe in the fumes of the ether.

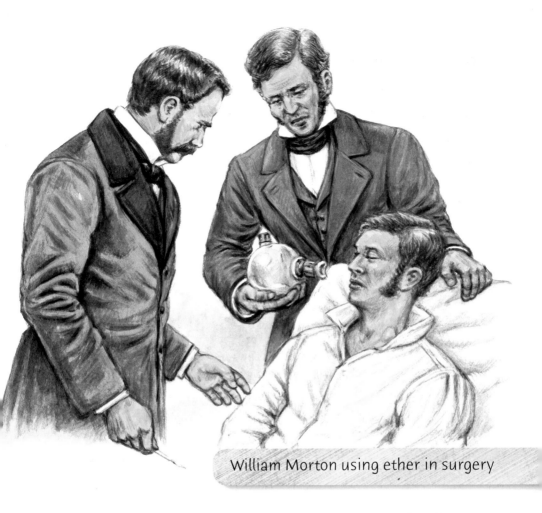

William Morton using ether in surgery

Morton found that if he gave a patient ether, he could pull out teeth without the patient feeling pain. He demonstrated ether at the Massachusetts General Hospital in Boston, USA, by cutting a tumour from a man's neck in front of medical students and surgeons.

Ether quickly became popular with people who needed surgery.

But ether has nasty **side effects**. It hurts the throat and causes headaches and sickness. It also catches fire very easily, making it dangerous to use.

Doctors tried other chemicals and found chloroform, another liquid anaesthetic. It sends people to sleep quicker than ether and is easier to use. Chloroform was used a lot during the American Civil War from 1861 to 1865 in operations on wounded soldiers.

chloroform being used in an operation on a soldier in the American Civil War

In the 1800s, new medicines weren't tested carefully before they were used on patients, and some people died unexpectedly after being given chloroform. It took many years for doctors to work out that chloroform caused the deaths. We now know that chloroform acts as a poison and damages many parts of the body.

Doctors searched for anaesthetics that were safer than chloroform. Several different gases are used as anaesthetics in hospitals today.

There are also liquid anaesthetics which are injected into the patient's blood.

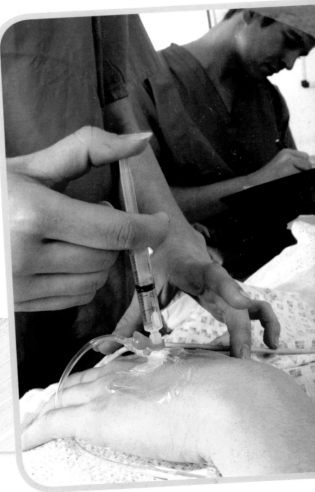

An anaesthetist injects liquid anaesthetic into a patient. They work quickly and can be controlled better.

Both ether and chloroform put patients to sleep, but today there are also local anaesthetics which make an area of the body numb. The patient can't feel pain in that part, but stays awake. The first local anaesthetic was used as eye drops in 1884 to make eye surgery more comfortable.

If you have a nasty cut that needs cleaning and stitching, you might have a local anaesthetic to stop it hurting while a doctor works on it.

But if you need an operation on your insides that involves cutting you open, you have a general anaesthetic to put you to sleep.

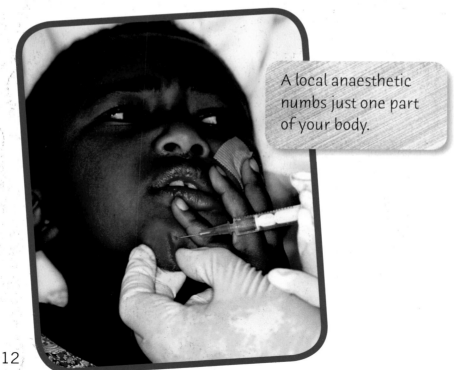

A local anaesthetic numbs just one part of your body.

A general anaesthetic puts you to sleep.

All clean

Anaesthetics allowed surgeons to operate on people's insides. But opening up the body meant germs could get into it.

A wound can easily become infected if it's not kept clean. Modern hospitals use **antiseptics** to kill germs in the operating room and on surgical tools, and **antibiotics** to kill germs inside the body.

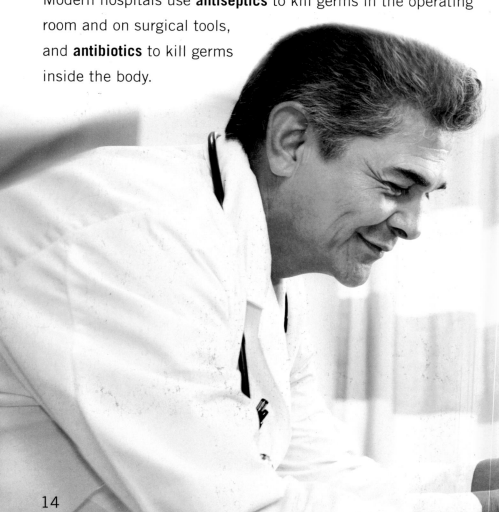

Tools for the job

A thousand years ago, Scottish soldiers covered their battle wounds with moss. The moss soaked up blood, and natural antibiotics in the moss stopped wounds going bad.

Moss bandages were used again in the First World War when there wasn't enough cotton to make normal bandages.

a moss bandage used in the First World War

Battle wounds easily become infected when weapons are dirty. Ambroise Paré was a French army surgeon. In 1536, he found a new way of treating injured soldiers. Usually, wounds were burnt with boiling oil to stop the bleeding, but the shock often killed the patient. Paré ran out of boiling oil and tried treating injuries with a cold mixture of egg yolk, oil and **turpentine** instead.

Paré's mixture was similar to one used for less serious wounds. To Paré's surprise, the soldiers felt less pain and more survived. His mixture prevented germs growing in the wound, though he didn't know that.

Tools for the job

For many centuries, people have used maggots to eat away rotted flesh, leaving a wound clean. Some modern hospitals are now using maggots again for this.

Three hundred years after Paré's discovery, Ignaz Semmelweiss worked in a hospital in Vienna, Austria. He was alarmed by the large number of women who died after having babies, so in 1847 he decided to investigate.

He found that women were more likely to die when doctors went straight from examining dead bodies to delivering babies without washing their hands. When he insisted they wash their hands, the number of deaths dropped.

But doctors refused to believe that they were accidentally killing their patients and ignored Semmelweiss – so patients continued to die.

Tools for the job

Surgeons did not wear special, clean outfits until the 1930s. Before, they operated in ordinary clothes, which became encrusted with blood. They were proud of their filthy clothes, which showed they did lots of operations! The dirty clothes were dangerous for patients, though, as they carried germs.

Semmelweiss didn't know about germs – he just noticed a link between dirty hands and deaths. In the 1860s the French scientist Louis Pasteur explained that link. He realised that food goes bad because of tiny living things called **bacteria**. He soon found that bacteria also cause some illnesses.

Louis Pasteur discovered bacteria while investigating how soup goes bad.

At the same time, English surgeon Joseph Lister was very concerned at the high rates of infection after surgery. Hearing about Pasteur's discovery, he realised that germs were getting into wounds and causing infection.

Lister knew that carbolic acid was used to clean sewage and stop bad smells. He tried soaking dressings for wounds in carbolic acid and operating on patients in a spray of carbolic acid. Death rates fell dramatically because the carbolic acid worked as an antiseptic.

Joseph Lister sprayed carbolic acid over his patients' whole bodies during surgery to kill germs.

ːill germs outside the body, but infection happens
ɡet inside the body from the air, dirty water,
ɹrgical tools.

Antibiotics are medicines to kill bacteria in the body. The first
modern antibiotic, penicillin, was discovered by accident in
1928 by the Scottish scientist Alexander Fleming.

Alexander Fleming

Fleming left one of his experiments
while he went away on holiday.
Later, he discovered that a chemical
produced by the mould he was
growing had killed the bacteria.

We now have many different antibiotics, used to kill different bacteria. But some bacteria are changing and are no longer killed by existing antibiotics. Scientists constantly look for new antibiotics.

Keeping hospitals very clean is even more important as antibiotics work better in clean conditions. Medical staff scrub themselves with soap and wear sterile clothes. Instruments are sterilised by boiling or radiation, and surfaces are all cleaned thoroughly with antiseptics.

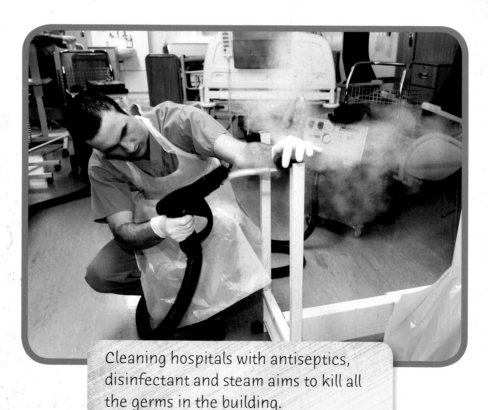

Cleaning hospitals with antiseptics, disinfectant and steam aims to kill all the germs in the building.

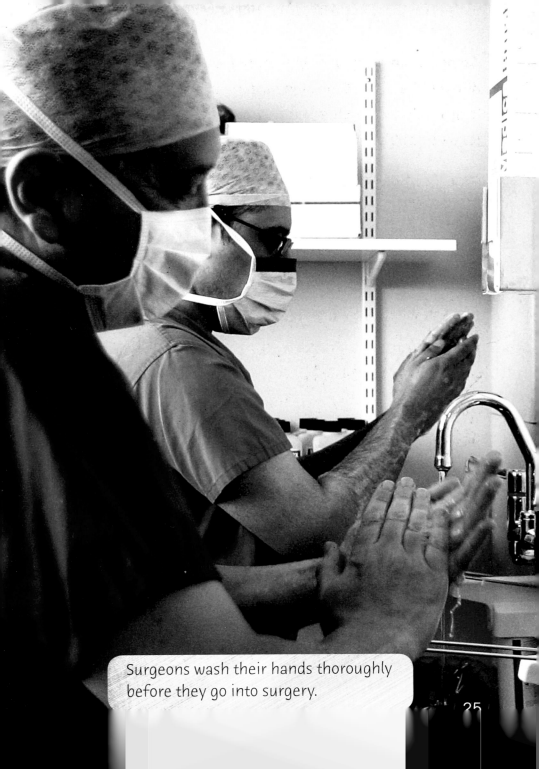

Surgeons wash their hands thoroughly before they go into surgery.

Stitched up

Closing wounds helps to prevent infection and aids healing. Something that holds the cut edges of a wound together is called a suture.

Even ancient cultures stitched wounds, using bone or metal needles. People have used plant fibres, hair or strips of animal gut, **nerves** or blood vessels as thread.

In ancient times, spines from cactus plants were sometimes used to hold together wounds.

Tools for the job

Sutures made from catgut – twisted strips of animal gut – have been used for at least 2,000 years. Catgut dissolves in the body, so stitches do not need to be removed. Most modern sutures are made of artificial materials.

In some parts of Africa, people pushed thorns through the edges of a cut, then pulled them together with plant fibres or animal gut. In early India and South America, a doctor made an ant or beetle bite the edges of the wound together then twisted off its body, leaving the jaws as a suture!

The strong jaws of an ant can hold a cut closed.

27

Before stitching the edges of a wound together, doctors often need to seal cut blood vessels to stop the bleeding.

Doctors used to burn wounds with hot metal, tar or oil. In 1536, Ambroise Paré found a gentler method: he tied threads around the ends of cut blood vessels.

Paré working on a patient on the battlefield

Sometimes, rather than sealing the end of a cut blood vessel, the two ends need to be stitched back together so that the blood flows around the body again. In 1894, the president of France was stabbed to death. Doctors could not save him because they did not know how to stitch blood vessels. His death inspired the surgeon Alexis Carrel to learn how to make very small stitches. He took lessons from an expert in **embroidery** and practised on animals until he could stitch perfectly.

Alexis Carrel learning embroidery

Carrel's techniques are still used today. They make very delicate operations possible, such as reattaching body parts that have been cut off. In this type of surgery, cut blood vessels and nerves are stitched back together, as well as muscle and skin.

In modern hospitals, wounds can be stitched, or held together, with sticky strips similar to plasters, metal clips like staples, or even with special skin glue. Skin glue and sticky strips are used on small wounds. Larger wounds need strong clips.

Stitches hold the edges of a wound together while it heals.

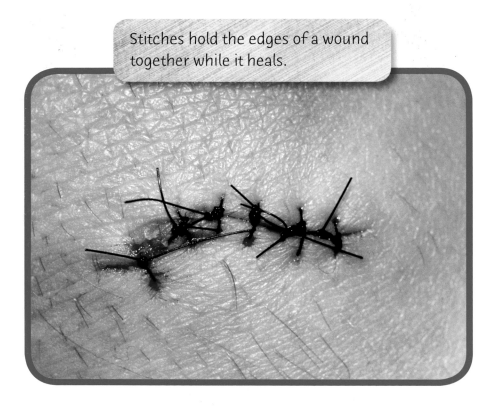

Sticky strips can be used to hold small wounds closed.

New parts

If a wound is very wide, it's not possible to draw the edges together for stitching. Instead, the hole is patched with new skin, called a graft.

a skin graft that has started to heal

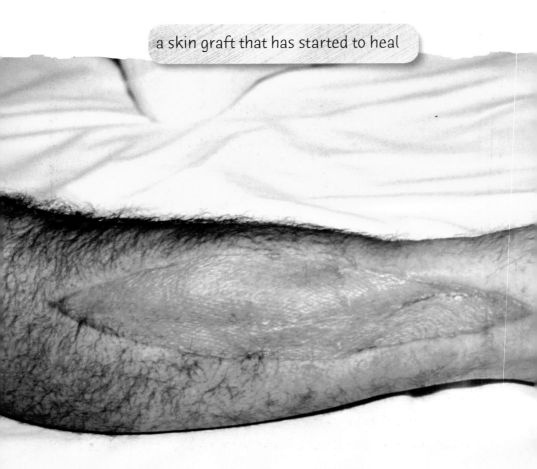

The first doctor to use skin grafts was the Indian, Susruta, about 2,500 years ago. Susruta rebuilt noses that had been cut off in battles or as a punishment.

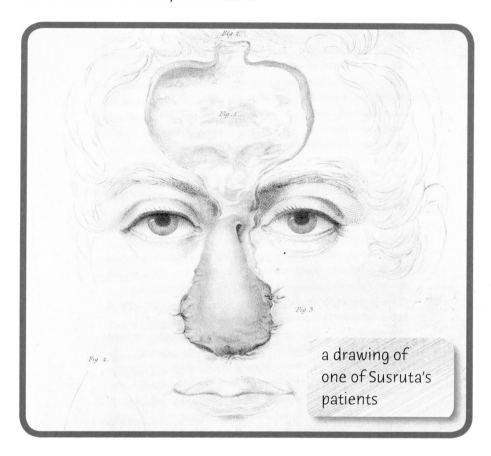

a drawing of one of Susruta's patients

To make a nose, he used two hollow reeds for nostrils, then cut skin from the patient's forehead, which he folded over to cover the new, fake nose. The skin stayed attached to the forehead while it repaired, so that it still had a blood supply.

During the First World War, many soldiers had terrible injuries to the face. The surgeon Harold Gillies developed new techniques to help them. He studied a soldier's face, then made a plaster model of how he wanted it to look. Using muscle and sometimes bone from elsewhere on the soldier's body, he built up the face until it matched his model. Then he grafted skin over the reconstruction.

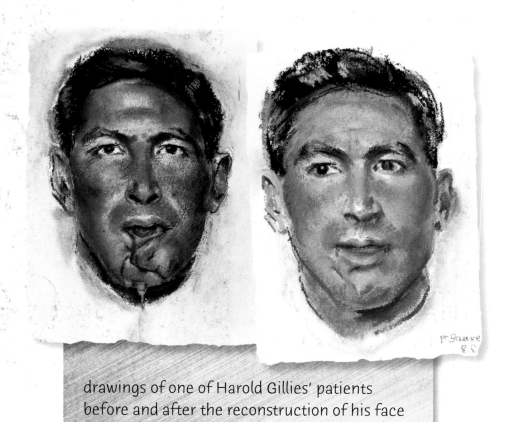

drawings of one of Harold Gillies' patients before and after the reconstruction of his face

When people are badly injured, like Gillies' soldiers, they lose a lot of blood. Doctors tried to tackle this by giving patients blood from other people. Early attempts rarely worked – often, the patient became more ill.

The problem was solved in 1901. Karl Landsteiner discovered that blood is of different types, called groups. If a patient is given blood from the wrong group, the blood forms **clots** and the patient can fall ill or die.

Once doctors understood about blood groups, they could give blood transfusions and carry out longer operations, including organ transplants. A transplant replaces a body part that doesn't work properly with one from someone else, called a donor. Often, the donor is someone who has died.

Karl Landsteiner's discovery of blood groups made successful transfusions possible.

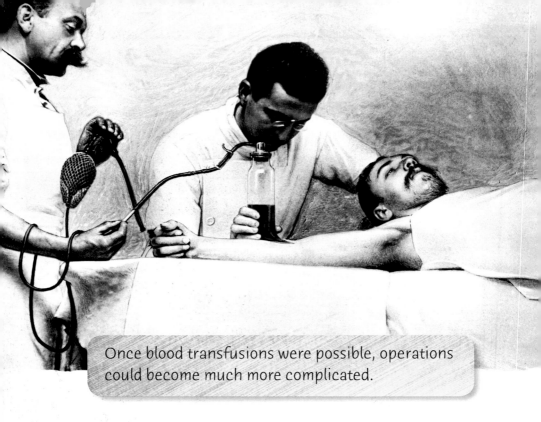

Once blood transfusions were possible, operations could become much more complicated.

Doctors tried transplants between animals and people, and then between people. The first successful transplant was carried out by an Austrian eye doctor, Eduard Zirm, in 1905. He put the **corneas** of a young boy into the eyes of a man blinded in an accident. The man regained sight in one eye after the operation.

Early transplants rarely worked because the body turned against the new body part, fighting against it like it fights germs. Then scientists developed medicines to stop this happening.

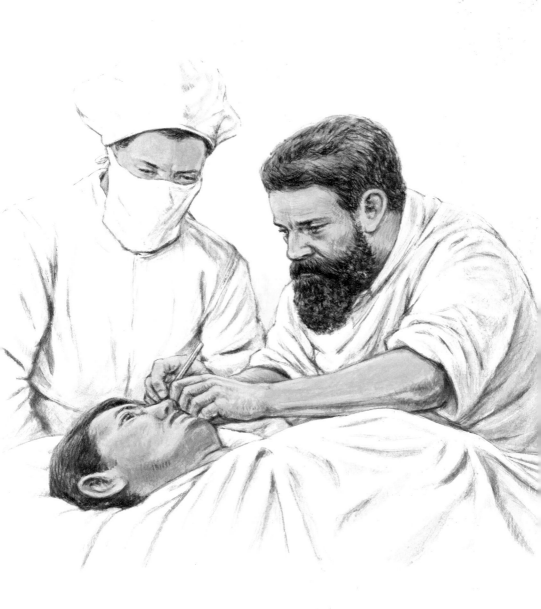

Eduard Zirm performing a cornea transplant operation

Transplants of internal organs started in the 1960s.
Before they could happen, doctors had to solve many problems.
They needed anaesthetics and antibiotics; they had to be able
to suture blood vessels and nerves; they needed to know
about blood groups; and have medicines to stop the body
rejecting new parts.

Now doctors can replace many body parts, including heart,
lungs, hands and even faces. But there are not enough donors
for all the patients who need new parts.

This patient was the first person to
have a whole hand transplanted.

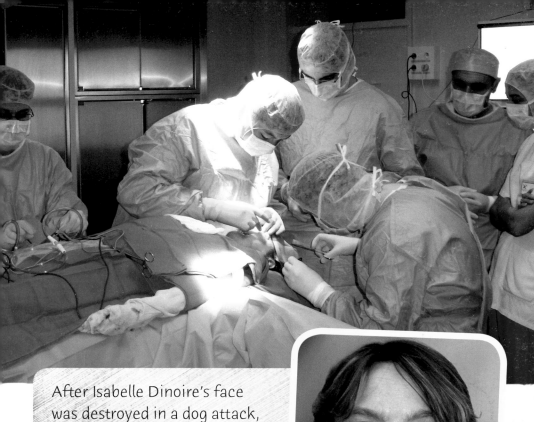

After Isabelle Dinoire's face was destroyed in a dog attack, she had the first ever face transplant.

Scientists are starting to grow animals with body parts that the human body will accept. Some people are uncomfortable about growing animals just for transplants, and some don't like the thought of using animal parts in humans.

Forging ahead

Surgery has come a long way in the last 150 years. What does the future hold?

Already there are surgical robots that can do more detailed work than a human hand. The robot is controlled through computers by a surgeon. A microscope and video camera show the surgeon what is happening.

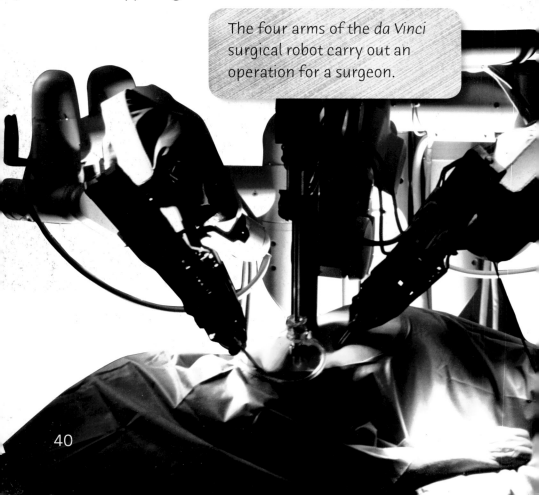

The four arms of the *da Vinci* surgical robot carry out an operation for a surgeon.

In the future, surgery might even be able to be performed on people in space.

In the future, surgeons might be able to use robots to operate on people far away, in ships, or even on spacecraft. Expedition teams would take the surgical robot with them in case of an emergency.

Lasers are very intense, narrow beams of light. They can "cut" flesh by burning in a very thin line. The heat seals the ends of blood vessels, stopping the patient bleeding as they're cut. As no tools touch the body, the chance of infection is low. Lasers are already used in eye surgery and to remove tumours.

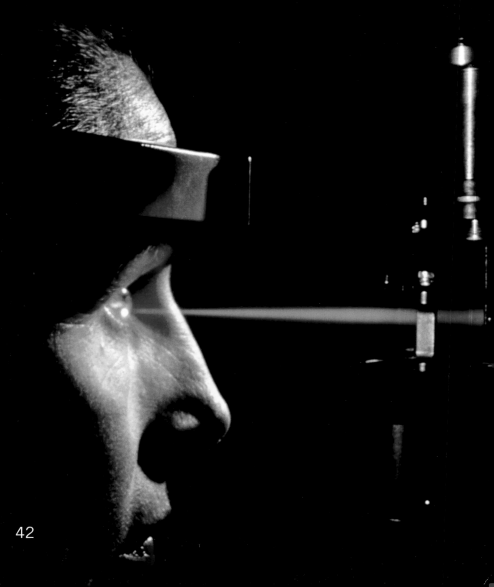

Nanotechnology uses very tiny equipment, so small it can only be seen with a microscope. Scientists are working on nanobots that they hope will be able to move inside the body to carry out treatments or deliver medicines just where they are needed.

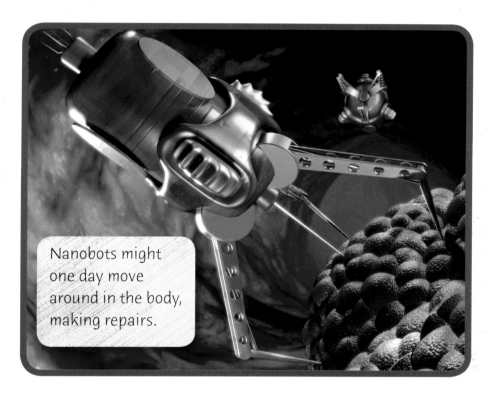

Nanobots might one day move around in the body, making repairs.

Some of the surgery of the past looks horrifying to us now, but medical science has improved hugely over the last 150 years. Perhaps in the future new, better treatments will make our current surgery look very basic. Who knows what surgeons will be able to fix in another 150 years?

Glossary

antibiotics   medicines that kill germs inside the body which can cause disease

antiseptics   chemicals that kill germs on the body which can cause disease

bacteria   very tiny living things, some of which can cause disease

clots   lumps formed by liquid going thick and clumping together

corneas   transparent layers at the front of the eyes

embroidery   very small sewing stitches

evaporates   liquid turns into a gas because of heat

infection   disease caused by germs entering a wound

nerves   long, thread-like fibres that carry information to and from the brain and spinal cord

side effects   results caused by taking medicines

tumours   lumps caused by unusual tissue growth in the body

turpentine   a strong-smelling liquid

Index

How surgical problems were solved

Problem	Then
Pain 	• no good painkillers • patients could die of shock • some refused surgery because of the pain
Infection 	• wounds not cleaned so germs got in • doctors didn't wash their hands so germs spread
Wounds 	• didn't know how to stitch blood vessels together
Wide wounds 	• couldn't repair wide wounds or replace internal organs